Her paper plane zips up... hovers in the air for a second...

then

CRASHES

to the

floor.

Zara's gran appears in the doorway. "Can I try?" she asks.

Her fingers fold the paper like MAGIC...

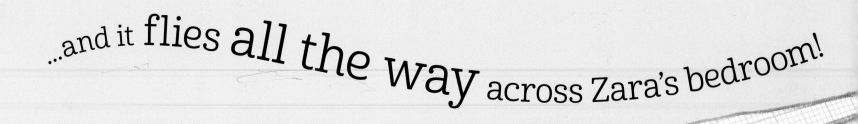

...and it flies **all the way** across Zara's bedroom!

"How did you do that?" Zara asks.

"I'll show you later," says Gran. "Right now, we've got things to do!"

AN ENGiNEER LIKE me

WRITTEN BY

Dr Shini Somara
WITH *Catherine Coe*

ILLUSTRATED BY

Nadja Sarell

wren & rook

Zara is curious about everything!
This morning she saw a plane fly past
her bedroom window, and decided she absolutely
HAD to make one of her own.

"Why do we take the lift?" asks Zara as they get in.

"Because it's tiring going up and down stairs!" Gran says. "Lifts get us to where we want to be without using up much of our energy."

"But how does a lift work, Gran?"

Electric motor
The motor moves the lift and the counterweight up and down.

Pulley
A wheel with a groove for the cables to run through and change direction.

Cables
Metal ropes that support the lift.

Counterweight
A metal weight that balances the weight of the lift.

"The lift uses cables around a pulley," Gran explains. "These are powered by an electric motor.

When the motor moves one way, the lift goes up. And when it turns the other way, the lift goes down!"

Outside, another plane is taking off.

It's HUGE and looks very heavy compared to the paper plane Gran made fly across Zara's bedroom!

Electric motor
This lifts the load.

Jib

Trolley
A machine to move the load along the crane's jib.

Cab
Where the operator controls the crane.

Hook

Counterweight
Large concrete weights to balance the load the crane is lifting.

Tower

They pass a construction site busy with vehicles and people.

"How can that crane lift something so heavy?" Zara asks.

"Ah, cranes use counterweights to even out their load. A bit like a seesaw needs two people at either end to balance!" explains Gran.

"And why is that truck pushing so much sand about?" Zara asks, pointing.

"That's a bulldozer. It's used to move sand or soil from one place to another with its big, wide blade."

Blade

Track

Zara spots a plane-shaped shadow on the ground. "How do planes fly, Gran?"

"Aha, you'll have to wait and see," Gran says mysteriously.

Walking on, they pass a fun fair. A roller coaster zooms along, and then it turns upside down!

"Gran, how do the roller-coaster cars stay on the track when they go upside down?"

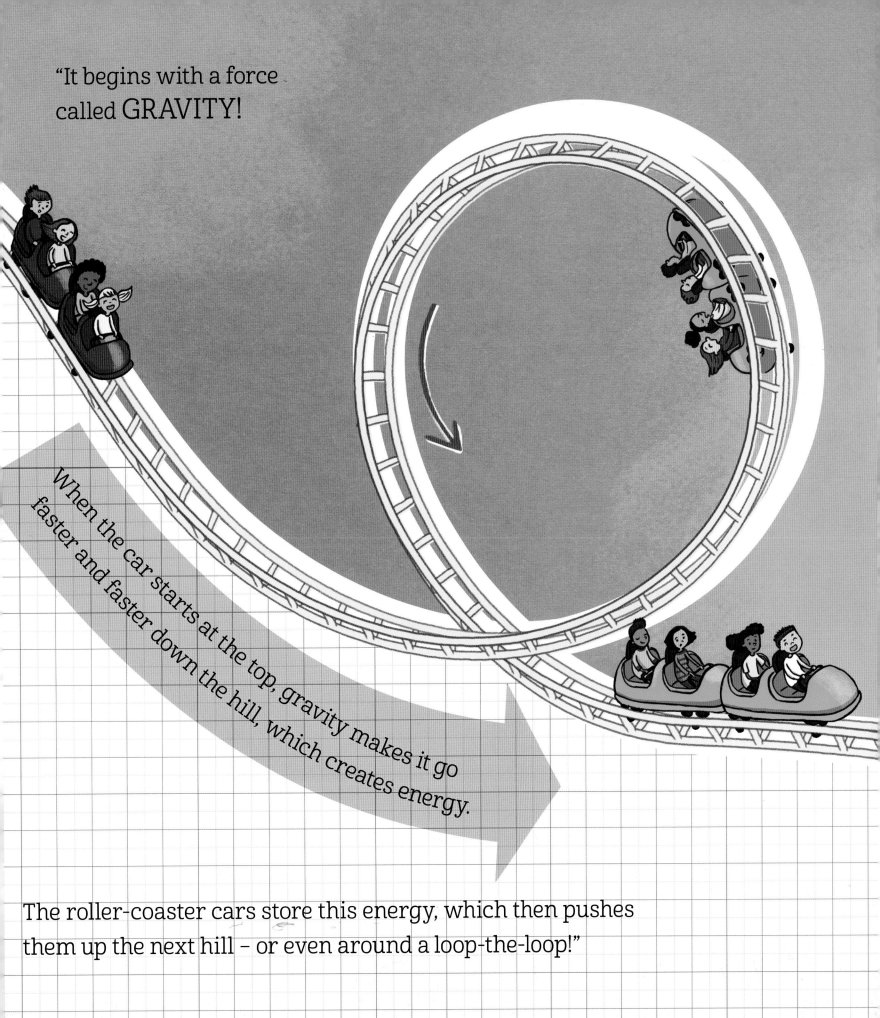

"It begins with a force called GRAVITY!

When the car starts at the top, gravity makes it go faster and faster down the hill, which creates energy.

The roller-coaster cars store this energy, which then pushes them up the next hill – or even around a loop-the-loop!"

When Zara and Gran reach the shop, they take the escalator up. Zara stares at the moving steps, wishing she could see what was underneath them.

"How do escalators work, Gran?"

Electric motor

Step chain
A motor-powered chain that pulls the steps along.

"They use a motor like lifts do, but the motor powers a big chain instead of a pulley. Just like the chain on your bike!"

Gran collects some books she ordered
and places them in her trolley.

"I know why you brought your trolley,"
Zara says. "It's much easier to carry heavy
things by pulling them on wheels!"

During a well-earned break at the shop's café, Zara wonders, "What's Wi-Fi for, Gran?"

"Wi-Fi sends information across the world without needing wires! It uses things called RADIO WAVES instead."

An American actress called HEDY LEMARR helped to develop the use of radio waves. Along with her friend GEORGE ANTHEIL, she created something called the 'Secret Communications System'.

By using radio waves, it sent information in an unbreakable code. The military later used it to send top-secret messages. That way, enemies couldn't understand them!

"Hedy Lemarr sounds clever!" Zara says.
Gran nods. "She was a great engineer and loved solving problems!"

Waiting for their bus home, Gran points at the cars driving past. "Chances are, at least one of those cars was made by another great female engineer!"

When ALICIA BOLER-DAVIS was a child, she loved solving problems and understanding how things worked. If the iron or the washing machine at home broke, she'd figure out how to fix it!

And every Christmas Day, she was the one who put together all the new toys for her siblings, not her parents.

Alicia's teacher told her she should be an engineer, but she didn't know what that was. As soon as she found out, Alicia was certain she was going to be one.

She went on to work at the General Motors car company, solving problems so that cars ran better. She ended up being in charge of 150 car factories!

"Wow, she sounds like me. I love making and building things too!" says Zara.

"Talking of cars," says Gran, "did you know that cars were invented over 500 years ago? But it was only 100 years ago that the first one was actually made!"

"Huh?" says Zara.

"Well, it was really more like a go-kart."

Most people know LEONARDO DA VINCI for his paintings, but he engineered some amazing inventions too.

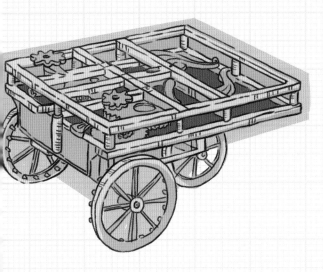

Leonardo saw that theatres found it hard to move heavy props around. So he solved the problem by inventing a cart that used springs to move without needing to be pushed.

He dreamed of flying, and drew the first parachute, which was a wooden pyramid covered with a piece of cloth.

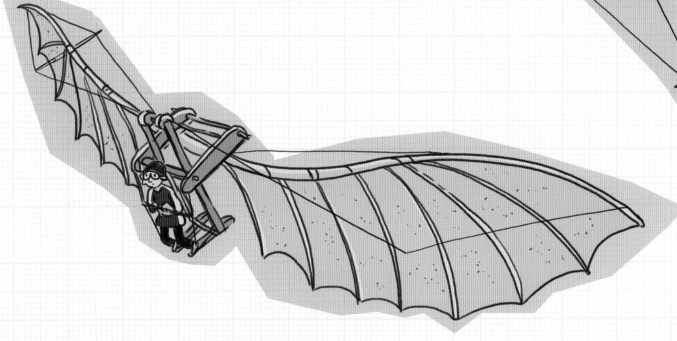

Leonardo also designed 'the winged flying machine', which wasn't so different from the planes we fly in today. But he never actually built it!

"See that skyscraper?" Gran asks.

Zara looks up...and up...and up...It's so tall, she can't even see the top!

It was designed by a man called FAZLUR RAHMAN KHAN. He wanted to find a way to construct tall buildings, but first he had to solve the problem that if buildings were too tall, strong winds and earthquakes could damage or even destroy them.

In 1963, Fazlur invented a new system, which meant tall buildings were supported on their outer edges. His system has been used for most skyscrapers ever since!

Still chatting away, Zara and Gran get on their bus.

Zara watches a man huffing and puffing up the hill on his bike. "Why is he going so SLOWLY, Gran?" she asks. "Our bus is much quicker!"

Air resistance
The force that pushes against a moving object.

Gravity
The force that pulls all objects towards a planet's centre.

"That's gravity again, pulling his bike down, plus air resistance, pushing against him! Cycling uphill is much slower than going downwards," Gran says.

"But a bus has an engine to power its wheels, which gets it up the hill much quicker. That cyclist only has his legs to power his bike.

Come on, we're getting off. We've got one more place to visit before we go home!"

"We're at the airport!" Zara shouts.

She's never seen a plane this close up.

A technician jumps out of a truck and pulls a long tube from it. She fixes the tube into a socket underneath the plane to fill it up with petrol.

"So planes use petrol like cars and buses," Zara says. "But Gran, how do they FLY?"

"Planes do use engines like other vehicles, but the wings are very important too.

They're AERODYNAMIC, which means that air moves fast over the top of them, creating a powerful force that pushes the plane upwards. Incredible, right?"

"How do you know so much about planes, Gran?" Zara asks.

"I design them. I'm an ENGINEER,
just like the people I told you about earlier!

It's the best job! I get to make new
things and solve problems.

Being an engineer is all about sticking at it –
trying and often failing until you succeed!"

Zara smiles. "I just have one more question, Gran...

"How can I be an engineer like you?"

There are many different types of engineer, but they all observe everything around them with curiosity and wonder.

So take the time to stop, observe and ask questions about everything around you.

Why does rain run off some materials but get absorbed into others?

Why do hot meals eventually go cold?

When you drop things, why do some break and others bounce?

A better understanding of the world we live in will help you to improve, change or even create solutions to problems yourself.

That's what engineers do best!

How do engineers solve problems?

Let's say you're trying to drop an egg from a height without breaking it. Engineers will build, test and experiment with some ideas to solve the problem.

What could you make from materials you have lying about at home?

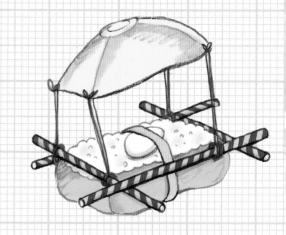

Cardboard, paper and plastic often gets thrown away at home, but engineers reuse these materials to invent and create models.

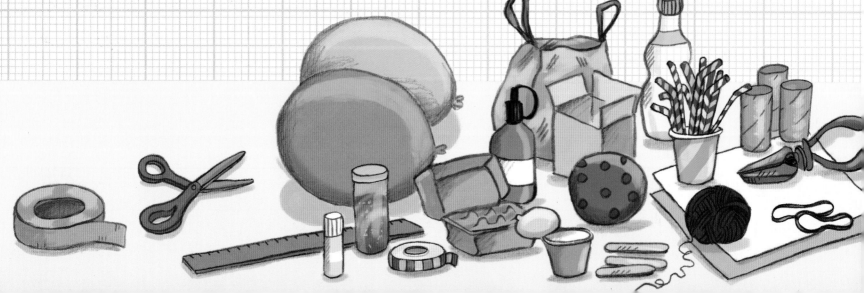

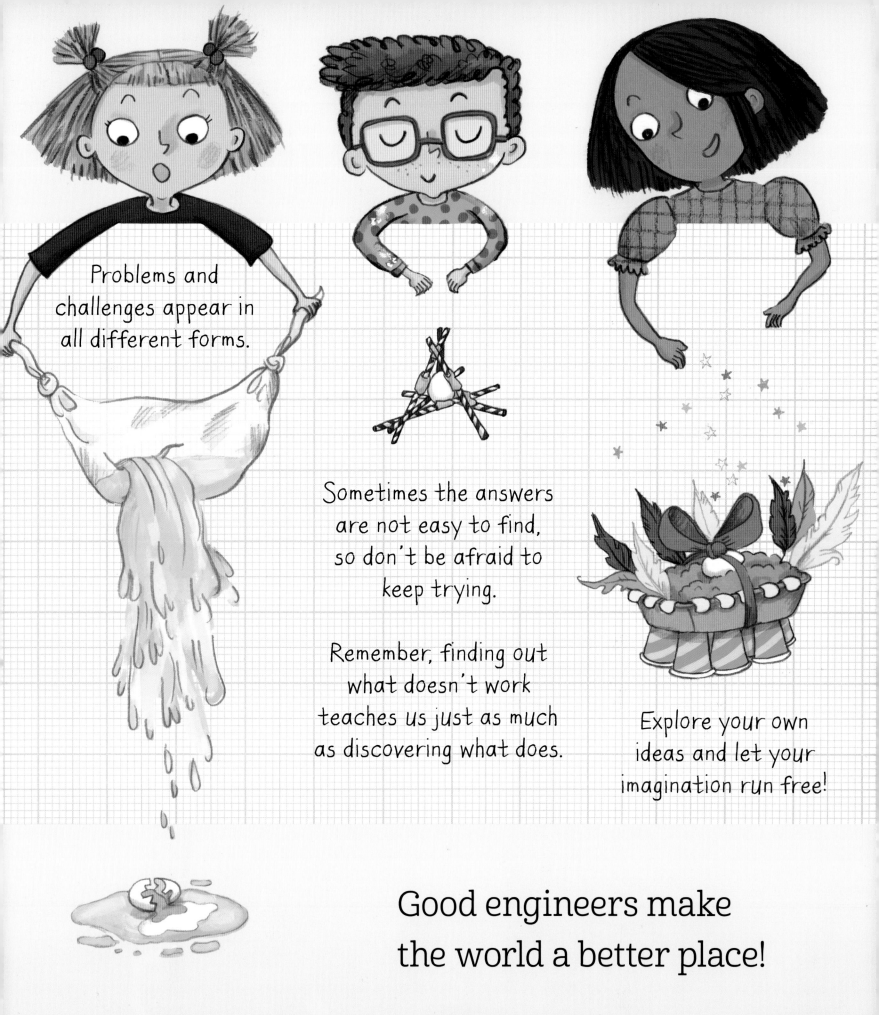

Problems and challenges appear in all different forms.

Sometimes the answers are not easy to find, so don't be afraid to keep trying.

Remember, finding out what doesn't work teaches us just as much as discovering what does.

Explore your own ideas and let your imagination run free!

Good engineers make the world a better place!

To Mum, Soraya, Sharlene and, of course, Dad –
my favourite engineer and first inspiration into engineering.
Thanks for all your support and love. – S.S.

To my son, the paper-plane and aviation expert
and my biggest inspiration – N.S.

First published in Great Britain in 2020 by Wren & Rook

HB ISBN: 978 1 5263 6199 8
PB ISBN: 978 1 5263 6201 8
E-book ISBN: 978 1 5263 6200 1
10 9 8 7 6 5 4 3 2 1

MIX
Paper from
responsible sources
FSC
www.fsc.org
FSC® C104740

Wren & Rook
An imprint of
Hachette Children's Group
Part of Hodder & Stoughton
Carmelite House
50 Victoria Embankment
London EC4Y 0DZ

An Hachette UK Company
www.hachette.co.uk
www.hachettechildrens.co.uk

Publishing Director: Debbie Foy
Senior Editor: Liza Miller
Art Director: Laura Hambleton
Designer: Barbara Ward

Printed in China

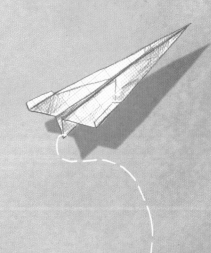